JUMPING SPIDERS

by Jaclyn Jaycox

PEBBLE
a capstone imprint

Pebble Explore is published by Pebble, an imprint of Capstone.
1710 Roe Crest Drive
North Mankato, Minnesota 56003
www.capstonepub.com

Library of Congress Cataloging-in-Publication data is available on the Library of Congress website.
ISBN 978-1-9771-3196-6 (library binding)
ISBN 978-1-9771-3298-7 (paperback)
ISBN 978-1-9771-5453-8 (eBook PDF)

Summary: Text describes jumping spiders, including where they live, their bodies, what they do, and dangers to jumping spiders.

Image Credits
Capstone Press, 6; Newscom: Mark Moffett, 23; Science Source: Scott Linstead, 24; Shutterstock: amirhamzaa, 14, common human, 8, Cornel Constantin, 10, Dustin Rhoades, 27, DWI YULIANTO, 17, kingfisher, 5, Marsan, 28, MR.AUKID PHUMSIRICHAT, Cover, Peter Yeeles, 1, 18, 19, Professional Fine Art, 12, Roman Kondrashov, 13, Ron Eldie, 21, Somyot Mali-ngam, 7, 22, Tomatito, 11, YSK1, 26

Editorial Credits
Editor: Hank Musolf; Designer: Dina Her; Media Researcher: Morgan Walters; Production Specialist: Tori Abraham

Table of Contents

Words in **bold** are in the glossary.

Amazing Jumping Spiders

Boing! What's that tiny animal hopping around? It's a jumping spider!

They aren't like other spiders. When they are scared or hunting, they jump! These little creatures can jump up to 50 times their body length.

Jumping spiders are a type of **arachnid**. There are more than 5,000 different kinds of jumping spiders. They are the biggest family of spiders in the world.

Where in the World

Jumping spiders can be found all around the world. They live on every **continent** except Antarctica. Many kinds of jumping spiders live in warm areas. But some live where it's very cold.

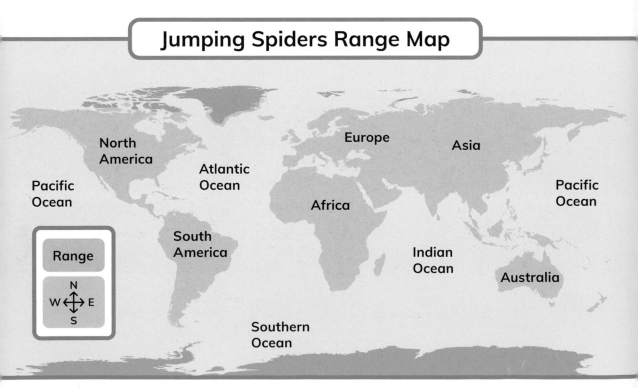

Jumping Spiders Range Map

North America

Europe

Asia

Pacific Ocean

Atlantic Ocean

Pacific Ocean

Africa

Range

South America

Indian Ocean

N
W E
S

Australia

Southern Ocean

Some kinds of jumping spiders build nests. They make thread called **silk**. The spiders hide under leaves or in cracks in trees. They use their silk to cover any openings. These nests are used for sleeping, resting, hiding, or laying eggs.

Jumping spiders live in many different places. They live in deserts and grasslands. They can live in wetlands such as marshes and swamps. They live in forests and mountains too.

You might even find jumping spiders when you play outside! As long as there is enough food and shelter, these spiders can survive almost anywhere.

Fuzzy Spiders

Jumping spiders have great eyesight. They have four pairs of eyes to see with! Their eyes help them see all around. They don't even have to move their heads.

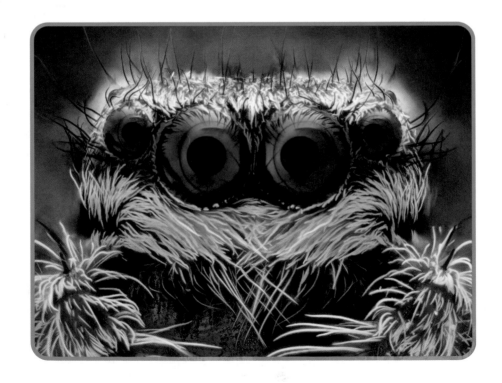

Jumping spiders have hairy bodies.
They don't have ears. They "hear" with
their hair. The hairs can feel **vibrations**.
The hairs also help them climb.

Jumping spiders can be many
different colors. Some are black,
brown, or tan. Others have stripes or
spots. These stripes and spots can be
bright colors. They include blue, red,
or yellow.

Jumping spiders are small. Most are less than 0.5 inches (1.3 centimeters) long. That's smaller than a pencil eraser! Females are usually bigger than males.

Jumping spiders have eight legs. Their front legs are longer than their back legs. The front legs are used to hold **prey**.

Their back legs are for jumping. But they are not strong. These spiders have a special way of shooting off the ground. They can make their blood flow quickly to their legs. Their legs suddenly straighten. Off they go!

On the Menu

A jumping spider spies a tasty bug. The spider slowly sneaks up on it. Pounce! It's time to eat!

Jumping spiders are not picky eaters. Most hunt during the day. They eat almost any insect they can find. They may also eat other kinds of spiders. Some types also eat leaves and **nectar**. Larger jumping spiders hunt birds and lizards.

Unlike other spiders, jumping spiders don't build webs to catch food. They attack their prey by jumping on them! Some kinds can blend in with their surroundings. It keeps them hidden. Their prey can't see them coming.

After these spiders jump on prey,
they bite them. **Venom** flows through
their fangs. It kills the prey. The spiders
hold prey until they stop moving. Then
the spiders eat them.

Life of a Jumping Spider

Most kinds of jumping spiders live alone. They only come together to **mate**. Males dance to attract females. They wave their legs in the air. They tap their legs. The female picks the best dancer.

Females build nests with silk. They lay their eggs there. Most can lay more than 100 eggs at once. The females stay with the eggs until they hatch. They protect the nest. Some will stop eating during this time.

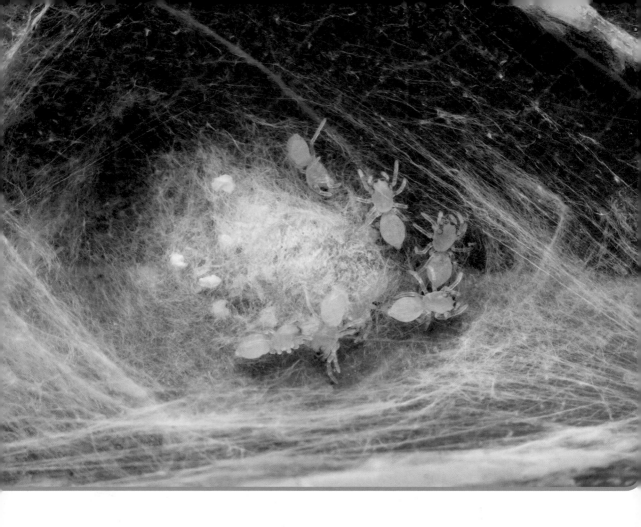

Eggs usually hatch after one to four weeks. The babies are tiny. They are called spiderlings. They look just like the parents. The baby spiders will stay in the nest for about a month. Then they chew their way out.

Some kinds of spiderlings leave on foot. Others fly away! This is called ballooning. They spin some of their silk and let it float. The wind catches the silk and takes them floating through the air. Wherever they land is their new home. The mothers usually die after the babies leave.

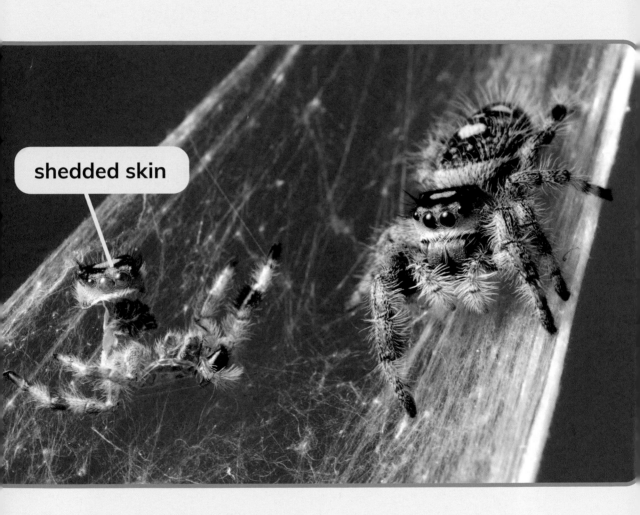

shedded skin

Young jumping spiders **molt** in order to grow. Their skin doesn't grow with them. They hide in a thick web and wiggle out of their old skin. They leave their old skin behind in the web. Jumping spiders molt five to six times before they become adults.

Molting is not only for growing. If a spider has lost a leg, it will regrow while molting.

Jumping spiders usually live only one to two years. Many die after mating and laying eggs.

Dangers to Jumping Spiders

Jumping spiders have a number of **predators**. Other spiders, wasps, and ants hunt them. Birds, frogs, and lizards do too. But these spiders have ways of staying safe.

One type of jumping spider looks and acts like an ant. This trick helps keep it from being eaten.

Jumping spiders also try to scare away predators. They wave their front legs in the air. They show their fangs. Sometimes they will bite predators and turn them into a meal instead!

Humans are also a danger to jumping spiders. Forests are being cut down. The spiders that live there lose their homes. People are working to save the forests.

Spiders are needed in nature. They are food for other animals. They also keep the number of insects down. It's important to protect them.

Fast Facts

Name: jumping spider

Habitat: deserts, grasslands, marshes, swamps, forests, mountains

Where in the World: every continent except Antarctica

Food: insects, leaves, nectar, birds, lizards

Predators: other spiders, ants, wasps, birds, frogs, lizards, humans

Life Span: 1-2 years

Glossary

arachnid (uh-RAK-nid)—a group of animals that includes spiders, scorpions, mites, and ticks

continent (KAHN-tuh-nuhnt)—one of Earth's seven large land masses

mate (MATE)—to join with another to produce young

molt (MOLT)—to shed an outer layer of skin

nectar (NEK-tur)—a sweet liquid found in many flowers

predator (PRED-uh-tur)—an animal that hunts other animals for food

prey (PRAY)—an animal hunted by another animal for food

silk (SILK)—a thin but strong thread made by spiders

venom (VEN-uhm)—a poisonous liquid produced by some animals

vibration (vye-BRAY-shuhn)—a fast movement back and forth

Read More

Gleisner, Jenna Lee. *Jumping Spiders*. Minneapolis: Jump!, Inc., 2018.

Higgins, Melissa. *Splendid Spiders*. North Mankato, MN: Capstone Press, 2020.

Rustad, Martha E. H. *Stunning Spiders*. North Mankato, MN: Capstone Press, 2017.

Internet Sites

DK Find Out!—Jumping Spiders
dkfindout.com/uk/animals-and-nature/arachnids/jumping-spiders/

Kiddle—Jumping Spider Facts
kids.kiddle.co/Jumping_spider

One Kind Planet—Jumping Spider
onekindplanet.org/animal/jumping-spider/

Index